The
Crab Shell Story

Patricia Masuda-Story, Psy.D., QME

ISBN: 978-0-578-20775-9
ISBN-13: 978-0-578-20775-9

DEDICATION

Dedicated to all my patients who have benefitted from The Crab Shell Story.

Also dedicated to my family and friends who have been patiently waiting for this story to finally come out in print.

ACKNOWLEDGMENTS

Special thanks to everyone at
Atomic Shrink Psychology, Inc.
&
Atomic Publications.

Special thanks to
Tatlin Campbell, Azja Campbell,
Mike Story,
Izabella Welle, and Margaret Riddle.

An extra special thanks to Tracy Grotefend
who really likes it when I include her
in my books and can't help but scream
at the top of her lungs in glee!

PATRICIA MASUDA-STORY, PSY.D., QME

INTRODUCTION

This story is <u>loosely</u> based on true events which took place in 1993. I have decided to write *The Crab Shell Story* as patients, friends, and family have asked me to do so on numerous occasions. Furthermore, I think the story will be beneficial to anyone who reads it; at least I hope.

THE FISH TANK

In 1993 I graduated from college with a Bachelor's Degree in Radio Television and Film Production, with an emphasis in Screenwriting. It was no surprise to me that two weeks after graduation, my dad insisted that I actually "find a job in that field." As I had spent what I believed to have been a ridiculously long time in school for most of my life, I wanted to take the summer off and make it mine. Therefore, I told my dad that I would start looking for a job in September. In a weird way, I think he was okay with this. He gave me $400 for graduation and told me, "Use it wisely."

That summer, I decided to spend every day at the beach. I absolutely enjoyed going with my friends to El Matador State Beach which was sandwiched between Malibu and Zuma in California.

Every day I would wake up at 6 o'clock and drive my little white Mitsubishi Galant all the way out to the ocean. I would walk approximately 1.5 miles to the caves and 1.5 miles back from the caves, and occasionally, I would actually dip into the water.

I was partial to low tide, because during low tide, you could actually see a myriad of colorful star fish. They weren't your typical orange starfish. They also came in red, purple, blue and green. I also very much enjoyed watching the sea anemones clinging onto rocks which littered the coastline. I found it quite interesting that there were little crabs that would climb up on these rocks and gently eat little particles that were attached to the sea anemones.

At times there would be feeding frenzies, and the crabs would have to fight another sort of crustacean that looked more like a sea bug of some kind. I don't know what they were, but the best way that I could describe them, they looked like gray or white little roaches that burrowed themselves in the sand, and when the tide came in, they would surface then rapidly burrow down beneath and leave little holes and bubbles of air which were soon erased by oncoming water.

On one particular day, I had this brilliant idea of what to do with the $400 that my dad had given to me for graduation. I decided that I would go down to this spectacular tropical fish store in Chatsworth. They were the largest emporium for everything that had to do with fish tanks and fish. I was amazed by everything that I saw. Every imaginable type of tropical fish was for sale. I finally decided that I needed a hundred gallon fish tank, which now I see really was ridiculous.

I bought two lion fish, various clown fish, a cow fish, and a whole bunch of other fish that I can't remember at this time. I just remember that everything was spectacular.

I recall the shop owner trying to convince me that I should actually get a much smaller tank and start with freshwater fish. His reasoning was that it was quite difficult to manage such a large tank with so many fish. He also stated that managing the water levels would be quite difficult, especially for "a novice." After much debate, I told him I would be "just fine." Against better judgment, he actually sold me all the things that I wanted.

MY DAD GETS UPSET

The day everything was delivered my dad seemed a bit taken aback. He answered the door and was quite surprised when two men brought this very large hundred gallon fish tank and asked where he wanted them to put it. After seeing the size of it, my dad decided that he did not want to have that anywhere in his personal space, or in the family's common space. Therefore, he had them take the tank up to my room.

Just to let you know, our house was built in a little bit of a weird way. I grew up in the Hollywood Hills, and the home was literally hanging off the side of a cliff. It was a three-story house with a very large long balcony. Though this is not important information at this time, this will be important momentarily.

That day, I came back from the beach and was

very happy to see my hundred gallon fish tank with all of the fish that I had purchased and accoutrements that came with it all. In particular, I had a light up sunken pirate ship, a little treasure chest with a skeleton that would reveal itself when it filled with air bubbles, gorgeous sea plants and a three inch layer of white lava rock.

The next day, as usual, I would go to the beach and come back home, and the day after that, I would go to the beach and come back home, and the day after that, I would go to the beach and come back home. This was my *routine* throughout the entire summer of 1993.

About two weeks after putting the fish tank in the house, I came back home and my dad said to me, "Hey, come here, I want to show you something."

"What now, dad?" Was my response.

"Let's go to your room. There's some sort of weird magical thing going on in there."

I remember putting my hands on my hips and giving him a really cross look. "What's the gag?" I asked.

We went up to my bedroom and my dad pointed to the fish tank.

"Look at that. I used to be able to look at this

tank and see fish here. Now, all I see is a screen of green."

"All right, dad, I get it." It was obvious that he wanted me to clean the fish tank... Immediately!

Luckily, I had purchased all types of fish tank cleaning equipment. As this was my first time cleaning the tank, I thought it was going to be a lot easier than it really was. However, that was not the case, and I didn't want to do an entire cleaning on that day. Therefore, all I did was just scrub out the glass. At least for the moment, that should have appeased my dad. He would be able to see the fish once the glass had been cleaned.

That night, I remember thinking there must be an easier way to deal with cleaning the fish tank. But what?

SEERSUCKER FISH

The next day, I decided to visit the fish guy in Chatsworth and see if he had anything that I could purchase that might help out with this task.

The fish guy stated, "Well, there's the seersucker fish. They'll eat the algae from the glass."

I was so excited to hear this. I asked how much they were, and he said they were $2.99. Considering they were so cheap, I bought four of them; one for each side of the tank.

When I got home, I was very pleased to see that the seersucker fish immediately clung to the glass and started creating trails of very clean glass as they ate away at the algae.

Thanks to the seersucker fish, they took off at least a week of cleaning. Without them, I would have to clean the fish tank once a week. At least now, I felt that I was getting a little break from such an arduous task each month.

DIRTY ROCKS

A few more days went by. I would go to the beach and come back home, go to the beach and come back home, go to the beach and come back home. Again, this was my regular routine during the summer.

On one of my arrivals from the beach, my dad said to me, "There's another magic trick going on inside your fish tank."

"Come on old man! What now?!" Was my response.

My dad and I went upstairs to my bedroom, and there, he pointed to the lava rocks and said, "Wow! All the white is gone! Now it's just green with lumpy browns!"

The task I had been dreading the most had

finally come to the point where I had to do it. Cleaning the white lava rock was no easy task, because I had to take all the rock from the third floor, down to the balcony on the bottom floor, and lay them out on a huge tarp so that the sun could bleach out all the algae and fish poop.

For those who don't know me, let me give you a little information. I am 4'9" tall. This served as a problem, because given my stature, it's not like I could actually take a huge bucket of rock at a time. No, not at all. What I ended up doing was filling up a huge bucket 1/3 of the way, because anything more than 1/3 of the way full was awfully heavy for me. In all, I remember this task used to take me 53 trips down the stairs, and when the lava rock was bleached out, 53 trips back up the stairs, three flights.

At the end of the day I was exhausted. There must have been some easier way to do this task. There just had to be. The following morning, I resolved to go see the fish guy again and see what he had for me.

THE CRAB

Once at the fish store, I told the fish man my dilemma. He crossed his arms, looked at me in a very strange way, and stated, "I have something, but I don't know if I want to sell it to you."

At this point I was shocked. I had already purchased a hundred gallon fish tank, an expensive filtration system, various fish and accoutrements. I couldn't fathom the idea of this man not wanting to sell me anything.

"It's not that I don't want to sell it to you," he said. "What I have, it's very difficult to handle. It has a very unique and interesting life course. It's environmental needs are very specific, and I think you might require something a little different. Maybe a cleaning service."

One thing I knew for sure, I didn't want to pay

for a weekly fish tank cleaning service. The going rate for that at the time was $25, and I thought that would cripple my budget. However, I was very interested in finding out about this particular *thing* that this man was talking about. I really wanted to know why he didn't feel like selling whatever it was to me.

"Again, it's not that I don't want to sell it to you," he said. "It's just that I don't think you would be able to *handle* this particular animal."

"Can you show me what it is at least?" I asked.

The fish man took me to a very specific corner of the store. There, he pointed to a saltwater hermit crab. My gosh this thing was beautiful! It had an absolutely gorgeous seashell on it's back, and it was neatly eating algae from the rocks within his tank.

"My God! That's beautiful! I want one! You must sell it to me!"

After much debate the fish man decided he would sell me the saltwater hermit crab. The price was $5.99. What was strange, though, was that the fish man was insisting that I pay $24.99 for a book about raising saltwater hermit crabs.

I remember taking the book in my hands and thumbing through it. It was a very thick book with lots of beautiful glossy photos. Regardless of how hard the fish man tried to get me to buy the book, I refused. I just didn't see the point in paying $24.99 for a book on the care and maintenance of a creature that was only $5.99.

When I got home I was very excited when I put the saltwater hermit crab in the tank. As I released him from the little baggie he gently floated all the way down to the bottom and immediately started rolling a small lava rock in front of his mouth, eating away all the algae. When he was done with the particular lava rock, he spit it out, and it was a bright, shiny, newly clean white rock. What I liked best about this guy was that he took off yet another week of cleaning from my monthly chore list!

THE HORROR! THE HORROR!

A little time went by. I still continued to go to the beach and come home, go to the beach and come home, and of course, go to the beach and come home… but one day was different.

I came home and my dad looked horrified. I asked him what was wrong, but he could barely speak. Eventually, when he caught his breath, he did let me in on his anguish.

"I saw horrific events in your fish tank today that I cannot unsee. I have got to go take a nap, because I cannot, for the life of me, believe what I just saw."

Naturally I rolled my eyes at my dad. It was clear to me at the time that he was exaggerating… or so I thought.

Once in my room, I was a little perplexed when I looked at the fish tank. There appeared to be two crabs in the tank. One with the seashell on top of his back running around happily, and one without the seashell, not moving.

After taking a closer look, I realized this darn saltwater hermit crab actually molted! In the moment, I thought that was awesome! I also thought to myself that there was no need for me to buy that $24.99 book to tell me that saltwater hermit crabs molt.

I was pretty happy in knowing that my crab had actually grown. In my head I was thinking that maybe now he would probably be able to clean my tank better and faster. I had nothing to base this on other than maybe maturity and size would allow him to put more effort into his life's work.

It was at that point that I did something that I now realize I never should have done... I removed the molt. Meaning, I removed the crab's former self from the fish tank.

I wish I had never done that.

PIRATES VS. EGYPT

The next day, I went to the beach as usual. When I got home, I noticed that the crab was acting up in the fish tank. In particular, he was running around like a jackass! I kind of figured that was what they did after molting. Heck! I didn't know! After all, I never did buy that book for $24.99!

For days the crab was running around the tank like a madman. Every day when I got home from the beach, I noticed he would go nuts going from one end of the tank to the other. He would do this all through the night as well. I would wake up in the morning, and he would still be running around.

One day about a week or so later, things changed. I came back from the beach only to find the crab had made many little pyramids in the fish tank. This upset me very much because I had a pirate theme going on, not Egypt.

So on that day, I flattened all the pyramids that the crab had made. I ruined all his work.

The next day, I went to the beach as usual, and when I came home, I found the same scene in the fish tank. The crab had made mound after mound of pyramids. Again, I flatten his work. This happened again day after day, after day, after day, after day.

Every day I would flatten and destroy his work!

About a week later, my dad came into my room and said that the family was going to Hawaii. I was so excited, because I had every intent of swimming with the real fish in Hanauma Bay in Waikiki.

My dad, was a bit of a smart ass. He suggested that I stay home and take care of my fish tank. He knew darn well that I was also a smart ass with all sorts of answers as to how my fish were going to be taken care of for two weeks while in Hawaii.

"Dad, don't worry about my fish. I can get these time release food capsules from the fish store."

My dad scratched his head and had a response, "But what about the filth in the fish tank?"

"Don't worry, dad," I said. "When I get back I will do a full thorough cleaning of the fish tank."

HAWAII

I absolutely enjoyed my two weeks in Hawaii. I actually went island hopping from Oahu, to Maui, to the Big Island, to Kauai. I snorkeled as much as I possibly could. As expected, Hanauma Bay in Waikiki was fantastic! I was able to actually swim and see wonderful fish such as snowflake eels, lots of clown fish, cow fish, and other fish. On one day I briefly was able to take a ride on a sea turtle.

My dad had business in Hawaii, so he didn't spend any time at the beach the way my mother and I did. My mother tried to get me to stay on the sand and sun tan with her, but I had no interest in that whatsoever. She didn't want me in the water because she thought I would drown. Mothers! they are so overprotective!

Night times were fun and exciting in Hawaii

as well. I really enjoyed going to a luau every single night for two weeks straight. While there, I actually learned how to spin fire, and that was the coolest thing I had ever learn in my entire life, up until that point.

I remember thinking about all the fish I wanted to buy when I got back home. All the fish that I had seen while snorkeling, I wanted one of each so that I could watch them swim around in my well oversized fish tank with pirate shipwreck theme.

My dad would come home from work and he would put up with all of my comments about buying more fish. After a while, I realized that he had tuned me out when he repeatedly kept saying,"Um-hum, um-hum, um-hum."

My mother wasn't too thrilled with any of the comments either. She too was sick and tired of my fish tank. Ever since I got the fish tank she repeatedly keep telling me that it was the biggest mistake I had ever made, and that she couldn't stand the smell, and she couldn't stand me going up and down the stairs with buckets of heavy rocks because it would allegedly "break" my back.

My last day in Hawaii I just decided to keep my thoughts to myself. However, I had every intention of going to the fish guy as soon as possible and buy a lot of fish.

BACK FROM HAWAII

When we got back from Hawaii, I was more than happy to clean out my fish tank. I knew it was going to be a complete disaster when I got home. But, since I had spent a lot of time swimming with tropical fish in their natural habitat, I was inspired, and I wanted my existing fish to have an awesome environment. I also wanted to make way for all the new fish I was planning on purchasing.

As soon as the taxi dropped us off in front of our house, my dad grabbed the luggage and placed them in front of the door. My mom fumbled for the keys. When she found the house key, she inserted it into the lock and turned.

The door made a unique and interesting pop sound; the type of sound you get from a door that hasn't been opened in quite some time.

When the door opened, this horrible stench overcame us all. It was horrific. It was God awful! It was from my fish tank, and we all knew it.

"Something is dead inside this house!" My mother declared.

"You're going to clean up that mess right now!" My dad demanded.

"Yes! Yes! That was my intention all along. I will get on it immediately after I go to the bathroom."

I really did have every intention of cleaning the fish tank immediately. In fact, I wanted to do it rather quickly so that I could go immediately down to the fish store before it closed for the night.

"There's something seriously wrong!" My mother was just not believing that it was only the fish tank that was causing that God awful stench. She was convinced that maybe somehow a strange animal had entered the home while we were gone.

My dad also seemed to think there was more drama involving the stench. "Maybe a raccoon or something managed to get inside the house," he said

We followed the trail of stink. As suspected,

the trail led directly to my bedroom. I opened my door, and that stench was even worse! At least ten times worse!

And then it happened… We all looked at the fish tank… our jaws dropped.

THE MOTHER OF ALL PYRAMIDS

We looked at the fish tank and could not believe our eyes. There was one monster sized pyramid in the middle of the tank. The saltwater hermit crab had apparently taken every single lava rock and created this amazing masterpiece.

Where was the hermit crab? I started to freak out because I couldn't find him. And the fish, they obviously were super pissed off, as they had very little room to swim around, and were all clustered up together at the top of the tank.

"Clean up this mess!" My dad demanded.

"Yes! Yes! That was my intent all along! Just leave me in peace so that I can do this!" was my response.

Both my parents left my bedroom. I then

opened up the hood of the tank. At that point I started to panic slightly because I saw a weird thing floating on the top of the water. It was the crab's large pincher claw, holding onto his other pincher claw. He clearly had torn off his arms!

I started to seriously freak out. *Where is the crab! Where is the crab!* That thought kept running through my head as I frantically tried to find the crab. And then, I found him... Right side of the tank... upside down... dead... His seashell next to him, filled with fish poop.

I cleaned the entire tank that night. I wasn't happy.

THE FISH GUY

The next day I went to the fish store and talked to the fish guy. I told him everything that had happened. I remember he crossed his arms not listening to me, and kept nodding his head, like he knew exactly what I was talking about. There was something mildly condescending about the look on his face.

"Let me tell you what you did wrong," the fish guy said. By taking out his molt, you took away his only ability to have closure."

"Closure?" I asked.

"Yes, closure," he said.

"I don't understand."

He uncrossed his arms, and now crossed his

legs and leaned back on one of the fishtanks. "You didn't want to buy the book. I really wish you had purchased that book. Yes, I know it was a little bit out of your price range, but at least there wouldn't be a deceased crab at this time."

I thought that statement was a little harsh.

The fish man continued, "I want you to imagine that you have to molt. Meaning, all your skin and all your muscles have to come off your skeleton. How would you feel about that?"

I thought about that for a minute and I started to feel really bad.

"I think I would feel really bad. I bet it's really painful," I said.

"Yes, I'm sure it is, but I want you to ask yourself, after you molted, what would you want to do with your molt?"

"Oh, that's easy. I would want to bury it." The look of shock hit my face. "Oh no! I took that away from the crab!"

"Yes, yes you did," the fish man said.

At that point I started to feel really, really bad!

"But what about all that running around that

the crab did after he molted?"

The fish man reposition himself and now crossed his arms again. "I want you to picture that you are inside of a fish tank. Or, that you are *trapped* inside of a fish tank. You just molted and you can't find your former self. What do you do? …You go nuts trying to find your former self inside this confined area."

"But what about all those mini pyramids?" I asked.

"Well, seeing that the crab could not find his molt, he had to do the next thing that he is supposed to do in nature. He had to create a pyramid to bury his former self in. But, after he did the first one, he realized he couldn't get any satisfaction. Therefore, he created another pyramid. And, when he was done with that pyramid he again did not feel a sense of completion and created yet another pyramid, and he did this again, and again, and again, and again, and again."

The fish man waited for a long pause and then continued. "And then you came home and destroyed his work. You did this day, after day, after day, after day."

I felt like an ass. I really wish I bought that damn book!

"But what about that big giant pyramid that was in the tank after I got back from Hawaii?" I asked.

"Oh, that's my favorite!" The fish man said. "When you finally stopped playing the hand of God and disappeared for two weeks, the crab was determined to have closure. Therefore, he took every grain of sand and rock from the tank and created the mother of all pyramids. But you know what? He still realized that he couldn't have closure. So what do you think he did next?"

I had no idea. As it was, I was feeling nauseous and miserable, and all I wanted to do was go home and cry.

"Well, let me tell you what happens next," the fish man continued. "The crab wants closure, so he figures he needs to start from scratch. He's going to make himself molt again. But I have a question for you. How much time in between molting do you think a crab requires?"

I had no idea and I certainly wasn't going to open my mouth under any circumstances. Therefore, there was this extremely long pregnant pause. A very long, uncomfortable, pregnant pause.

The fish man repositioned himself once again. "Apparently, saltwater hermit crabs molt once a year or once every two years. They certainly do not molt a month or two right after molting."

I tried so hard not to cry, but I failed. There was a paper towel rack nearby, and the fish man pulled a leaf and handed it to me.

"But it gets worse. Do you know how they molt? They take their big pincher claws and pull their shell right off. Well, this crab had really new arms. I'm sure they were quite tender. But he wanted closure so badly that he pulled, and pulled, and pulled, until he pulled his arms off. Now what do you suppose happens when you pull your arms off?"

"You die!" I said with tears in my eyes.

"Yes, you die."

I don't know how long I cried for, but I think I used all of this man's paper towels.

"What do we do if this happens again?" I asked.

"Again?! Are you kidding me?! After this is there going to be an again?!" The fish man was surprised that I would even say such a thing.

"No, no, let me explain," I said. "After I got my fish tank, one of my friends got really excited and got a saltwater fish tank of her own. The same problems I was having with my fish tank, she was having. She also bought seersucker fish, and she also bought a saltwater hermit crab. Well, she called me the other day and was telling me that her crab was doing the same stuff. My God, I feel horrible! Poor crab is going to die and it's all my fault!"

"No, no, don't worry," the fish man said.

He walked over to an accessory stand and pulled out what appeared to be a plastic toy crab. He handed it to me and said, "Have your friend put this in the tank. The crab is stupid. He won't know the difference."

WHY I AM TELLING YOU THIS STORY

We all have metaphorical crab shells in our lives. There is always something that we did or went through that we could not find closure to.

Sometimes we use people to resolve our closure issues, but these people are not the people we should be resolving these issues with. These are completely different people, and now we are trying to turn them into people they are not, in order for us to benefit. In doing this, we end up hurting a lot of people, not resolving our issues, and we continue to search and search endlessly.

I'll give you an example. Say you have two kitty cats. They have been friends for a while. They play with each other and enjoy each other's company. One day, they get into a massive fight. One cat will be triumphant and the other one will be defeated. The triumphant kitty cat will be able to move along with his life. However, the kitty cat who lost the battle, his personality will change. He may come into contact with other kitty cats and engage in battle unnecessarily. He may do this several times with several different kitty cats. However, he will never find closure, because the kitty cat that he needs to have closure from is long gone.

Here is another example. Let's say there is a man and a woman who have had a relationship for quite some time. Then, the relationship comes to an end. One will be victorious in their efforts to come to closure, and that one is usually the one who wants to end the relationship. The other one will be completely defeated, angry, hurt, etc. The defeated individual may then find comfort in another relationship, but they may punish their new mate for the crimes of their prior mate.

In other cases, they may actually try to *change* their current mate. Sometimes this can get out of hand, as they try to recreate their prior mate in their new mate, thus molding their subsequent mate or mates into the image or personality of their prior mate. This is never good. This is the equivalent of all those little pyramids that the crab created with the sand and rock... Empty efforts.

THE FIX

But how do we fix this? It's not as simple as handing somebody a plastic toy and saying, here, get closure with this thing. Nonetheless, we can learn from this lesson. We can at least stop the cycle of trying to recreate people in others or wrongfully accusing or punishing innocent people.

Once we identify our crab shells we may be able to actually create *psychological ceremonies* in order to overcome hurdles and gain closure. But that will be the subject matter of another book.

For now, the most important thing to do is to identify any existing crab shells that you may have. Create a list of them, and see how many ways you have tried to recreate people, events, or things, in order to gain closure.

ABOUT THE AUTHOR

Patricia Masuda-Story, Psy.D., QME is a licensed clinical psychologist in the states of California and Colorado. She is the CEO of Atomic Shrink Psychology, Incorporated. She has three locations where she sees patients in California: Lancaster, Glendale, and Big Bear Lake. She also has seven other offices where she works as a Qualified Medical Examiner in Psychology for the California Workers' Compensation system. These offices are located in: Riverside, Pasadena, Los Angeles, Ontario, Torrance, La Palma, and Orange. In Colorado she services patients remotely.

Dr. Story is also a romance novelist. Her most recent "spicy" novel is *Blue Flame*, which is available at Amazon in hard copy and on Kindle in electronic copy. This title may also be found in certain book store chains.

Made in the USA
Columbia, SC
20 March 2019